The Borrowed Life

Ritika Sharma

BookLeaf Publishing

Presentation by *BookLeaf Publishing*

Web: www.bookleafpub.com

E-mail: info@bookleafpub.com

ISBN: 978-93-95890-06-9

First edition 2022

This one's for each one of you reading.

ACKNOWLEDGEMENT

Grateful to everyone I've crossed paths with, for all the experiences that came my way.

PREFACE

What is life? That's perhaps the most difficult question we humans have been trying to find the answer to since the first one of us walked the planet. Have we found the answer? Will we ever? We don't know.

In the following pages, however, I've still made an attempt to uncover this mystery but not with calculation, with words wrapped in a strong scent of emotions, dipped in colourful waters of experiences, and decorated with the unreasonable logics of the heart.

From the doormat you walk every day to the world wonder you get to visit once in your lifetime, from the light bulb you replaced last night, to the loved one you lost forever - there are a lot of small things that make life. Let the following pages take you on a journey of recognition, appreciation, gratefulness, and celebration - for you always knew the answer to the biggest mystery of mankind - LIFE.

LOST AND FOUND

Since forever I feel,
You've been around.
Silent in crackling noises,
That made up my surround.
Since always I know,
You've listened to the implicit sound.
Worded the mute emotions,
Painted me in colours abound.
Since years before today,
You've comforted with warmth around.
Untangled the complex spaces,
Broke me free to rebound.
I lost you on the way,
As I braved the battleground.
And fought for self-concord,
From endless glooms that hound.
But amid infinite dark,
There dwelled a silver arch,
A renewed solace I then found,
Is this a new turnaround?
Or just a wave with a calming sound?
Touching the horizons of parched ground,
Or a comeback, I propound.

I AM A PEN

History says, I have carved ways,
For revolutions out of hays, to equal and better
days.
Hello, I am a PEN. I am mighty now; I was
mighty then.

People who hold me, are as vast as a sea,
Their intellect is the key, they show, what you
don't see.

I have played roles, in big freedom goals,
I have enriched souls, at times continents on
whole.
But today I am sad, for the holders that I had,
Are suffering for words against the bad, to my
grief this adds.

Yes, I am sad. Not for the change of forms,
But for the silent hypocritical storms,
In some minds like parasitic worms.

However, I am a pen - I am strong in end,
As nothing can ever bend, the power that I lend,
Power to keep and to send, to praise and to
offend,

Brighten truths that must transcend
The boundaries and blends, in each of us – foes
or friends.

Come what may, I am a pen, I will be mightier
now and then.
You may harm one or ten, but there is a world,
out of your den,
Where I guide, I am a PEN.

A SAGE's DEAL

Was broken, and shaken. Was someone's, but
not taken.
Said, put pains to bed. Noises in head, it's time
to be dead.
Packed bag, buried fag. Wore 'traveler' tag,
prepared for jet lag.
Crossed a sea, in far land to be. Find peace key,
and to open skies flee.
Walked unknown streets, colourful creeks. But
sadly bleak, recovery was meek.
Then came a sage, wiser in age. Saw the mind
cage, turned gloomy page.
Smiled, asked for hand. Tied across, a red holy
band.
Assured, all to be well. May in amity you dwell.
Thought, another wrist tie. Kept band, left with
sigh!
Month away, things fell in place. Surrounded me
an aura of grace.
In harmony, blessed I felt. With ease, difficulties
I dealt.
Looked at red tie. Bid despair goodbye.
New me, in mirror. Life and aims, clearer.
Wondered if it was real,
A blessing, a sage's pious deal.

That sorted the twined feel,
And, I live today with new zeal.

5

WHY DON'T YOU

When they say, WHY DON'T YOU:
Ask your husband to shave, direct your child to
behave.
Control your weight, and walk upright straight.
Why don't you:
Pray with rules, work tirelessly like mules.
Be more sorted and nice,
Bargain for every price?
Firm your voice, tell them:
I love his appearance; kid needs no clearance.
Am happy with my size, don't evaluate my
walk, you wise.
My prayer is about me and Him, work is not
someone's whim.
My discipline, not your trade, my spent is
different from the usual shade.
Can you live and let us enjoy?
The different looks, the untidy books,
The fluff of joy, and oh boy,
Our humane guise – a mix of laughter and cries.
Isn't this what life should be – flowing and most
of all FREE!

IF I FALL

I believe I am strong
but
You never know what life has in store
I have fought and taught but I am so different at
the core.
Storms could not stir me but
A light breeze has shattered me
Screams went ear-less but
A whisper often attracted me.
I stood firm in big troubles but
Petty episodes have broken me
I went against the tides but
Light showers have drowned me.
Yes, I am complicated but
This is what defines me.
So, don't catch me if I fall
I might break into a thousand pieces but
This is what completes me.

IT'S JUST THERE

Like the trees in the woods,
Like the heads in the hoods,
Like the cans in the coulds,
It's just there.

Like the truths in lies,
Like the lows in the highs,
Like the blues in the skies,
It's just there.

Like the colours in white,
Like the duller in bright,
Like in fact and in spite,
It's just there.

Like I am in you,
Like a solo in a crew,
Like a tear and a glue,
It's just there.

It's the life in the dead,
It's a destination in the tread,
It's a story in the unsaid,
It's always - just there!

I NEVER SAID

I will tie them in a rope,
Dot them with pearls of hope,
Design them for the hours of melting sun,
Place them on a platter made to cope.

I will say it all out loud,
Things I am and not allowed,
For some will hurt, some will cure,
So, I'll hide them in the darker cloud.

I've longing to say it all,
To make that forbidden call,
Pour out my heart and soul in bounty,
So, I'll need an endless empty hall.

These are things I never said,
They've stayed on a fragile, hidden thread,
Inside my dreams and on the wings of my
imaginations,
I wish I could say it all and move ahead.

THE DOORMAT

Dusty and old,
Used but bold,
Stepped on and told,
In snow and cold -
Be here and greet,
Even if I take off my heat,
Or see through you, neat,
You don't get to move or cheat,
Nor allowed to sigh and skip a beat,
You need to be intact,
I might shout at,
Or just sit back,
You be what you're best at,
Be a good doormat!

EVERYDAY'S A WOMEN'S DAY

As the world celebrates women today,
Do I have anything special to say?
While the sun shines, won't I make hay?
I would say, ummm well, 'nay'…
To celebrate women, I'll do it my way.
Don't need an occasion or an international day,
To say – "hey!
My dear women, the art of life that you slay,
The victory of every war and play,
The lessons that you learn and they,
The rules that you make and obey,
You're the boss – each day, every day

THE QUIET NIGHT

I heard her say,
That evening or day,
My darkness is threatening,
My sound is deafening,
I overpower the light,
Turn into black all that's bright,
I scream for the ones who listen,
Give dreaded thoughts the admission,
I am a fearless foe,
Cold and unwanted I am though,
But inevitable and slow,
I creep into evenings in a blow!
I heard her say that in whispers,
Oh, she sounded like lispers,
I told her, behold!
That's not how you're sold,
For lovers of solitude,
You bring emotions in a multitude,
You are a loved sight,
That's you, a quiet night!

THE LUGGAGE

I sat down to pack up,
Facing the clothes all stacked up,
Wish I could wrap the aroma of this house,
The far corners feel distant they pronounce.

The colours of the fall peek through the window,
Even the burnt grass that's always been so,
Wish I could box up all hues and shades,
As love in the new city is known to fade.

I look at the fog of memories in the air,
Says club me in your suitcase make it a pair,
The evening tea, the last streak of sunshine,
All want to come along, what do I decline?

Moving has its own shades,
Yes, I've been doing it for decades,
It still feels new every time I try,
To capture a home, masking a cry,
Why do I have to move again?
Why does this never cease, this pain?
Because a traveller is not allowed to stay,
His home is always one move away.

I AM HERE

I am here to fight,
Fight and vouch for what is right.
I am here to think,
Think and paint the world pink.
I am here to write,
Write a story of optimism day and night.
I am here to admire,
Admire those who hold the fire.
I am here to awaken,
Awaken for granted that is taken.
I am here for hope,
Hope that we get the strength to cope.
I am here to dream,
Dream and loudly scream
That
I am here for YOU,
Because tomorrow is a day that is NEW.
So, get up, fight, awaken and write,
Create a happier tomorrow, with all your might.

YOU'VE GOT

I am a keeper,
Or not.
I am sorted
I thought.
I am difficult,
Not sought,
I am running,
Never caught.
Be friendly,
I was taught.
They said, stand up,
I fought.
Hey, leave that,
But I bought.
I've obeyed,
Sometimes not.
I disappoint,
Often than I ought.
I need some lessons,
I need to be taught.
And I have a heart,
No one yet sought.
So tell me now,
What have you got?

STARED EMPTY

She stood on the door,
Stared with empty eyes,
May be she needed some more.

I handed her a bag,
Some food, some clothes,
Most of them missing a tag.

Her gaze piercing through,
I wondered what her story was,
And was any of it true?

I said, go away,
You came here yesterday,
Before that and even today.

She held her hand out,
Gave me back all I shared,
I could see on her far a very sad bout.

Not sure what she wanted,
Go, don't waste my time,
I was sad, hurt, and confused, so I taunted.

A few days passed and she came again,
With her kids and an old husband,
"I keep forgetting, that's the pain."

I was out of words to respond,
She came out to say 'thank you',
For offering me food that day and beyond.

After a chat, I kept wondering,
Why did I feel bad about that night,
Rain pattered and it continued thundering.

HOPELESS

My friend, hopeless is good!
An interesting quality to have, touch-wood,
One must try if one could
Because to be hopeless is so good!

It means you can't be repaired,
Can't be molded, Can't be shared.
What the world says, you never cared
At all the blames you sternly stared!

Hopeless is when you smile,
Even when the path is thorny for a 100 mile,
Though you sound foolish, that stays your style,
Every judgement you lower down in your pile.

You flow like an untamed sea,
Your dreams are what you want to be.
It is the chase that gives you glee
And in darkness, an illumination you see.

Senseless, dimensionless, endless,
Boundless, pointless, and useless.
They may say you are purposeless,
but tell them you are Hopeless!

If these words you often hear,
But they don't lessen your cheer,
My dear enjoy and be clear,
It is YOUR world, it is your Sphere!

DEFINING PLACES

I've been trying to define places,
Connecting their past with their present spaces,
My trick has worked wonders in all cases,
Created new stories with arts and aces,
Exemplified people and their journeys with utter
graces.

I've failed miserably at times as well,
I've never had some tales to tell,
Had no heroes or stars to sell,
How do you define dying and living hell,
And do that with panache, do that well?

Yes, I've tried defining places,
But have not always ended up in victorious
places.

I'VE LOST

I've lost a lot,
Some papers, a plot,
A schedule and a slot,
In someone's life, is that a lot?
I've lost many mornings,
Overlooked many warnings,
I've lost my fire,
The will to satire,
The ability to tire,
The zeal to retire.
I've lost the dusty nights,
The lovely sights,
The colours and the brights,
I've lost it all,
But I don't feel bad,
After all, losing isn't all too sad.
It makes spaces for the new,
Every morning has a fresh dew.

THE WALKING TREE

Have you seen a tree,
One that walks free,
One that talks and
Is on a fun spree!

It came to my lane,
It looked a little odd, but sane,
It looked at me and then again,
I wanted to ask a question in disdain.

Hey, aren't you supposed to be still?
How did you get off that hill?
Are you monitored or is the record nill?
How long you're grounded until?

It smiled and waved its branches,
I've walked the city and the ranches,
All I've noticed is a lot of absences,
Are the people of the city in any trances?

He spoke and walked past,
Like it a pastime for it and a blast,
It disappeared in my lane at the turn last,
I ran there to catch a glimpse, I ran fast.

It wasn't there - I came back,
I went back to my room, hid in my sack,
It was imagination, my mom said, "Jack".
"Come here, love, come back."

www.ingramcontent.com/pod-product-compliance
Lightning Source LLC
Chambersburg PA
CBHW061326140726
47998CB00007B/2569